QUICK GUIDE TO THE MLA REFERENCIN G STYLE

Easy Steps to Format Your Paper

2

MLA (Modern Language Association)

MLA style is the set of conventions for formatting papers and citations in most disciplines in the humanities.

In MLA style you briefly credit sources with Parenthetical References in the text of your paper and give the complete description of each source used in your paper in the list of Works Cited.

The recommendations in this guide are based on the 8th edition (2016) of the *MLA Handbook*. For more in-depth explanation of formatting and preparing works cited lists, please consult the 8th edition of the *MLA Handbook*, available at the Library Reference Desk, or the MLA Style Center, style.mla.org.

The instructor for your class is the final authority on how to format your References List.

PaperHacker Publications 2019

1. Formatting and Page Layout

1.1 General:

- 8.5 x 11-inch paper
- Double-spaced text
- Legible font 12 pt. (e.g. Times New Roman)
- 1-inch margins on all sides
- Indent:
  - Indent paragraphs 0.5 inch.
  - Indent set-off quotations 0.5 inch.
  - Use hanging indent 0.5 inch for citations.

1.2 Header:

- Includes student's last name, followed by a space with a page number.
- The upper right-hand corner.
- Flush with the right margin.

1.3 Page Numbers:

- Page number is placed in the header.
- Arabic numerals (1, 2, 3, 4, etc.).
- Start numbering pages from the very 1st page.

1.4 First Page Layout

- In the upper left-hand corner of the first page:
    - Student's name (Name and Surname)
    - Instructor's Name (Name and Surname)
    - The Course
    - The Date (Dates are written in this order: day, month, and year)
- Title:
    - Standard capitalization.
    - Centered.
    - Use quotation marks and/or italics when referring to other works in your title.
- Content:
    - Double space between the title and the first line of the text.
    - Italicize the names of books, plays, poems published as books, pamphlets, periodicals (newspapers, magazines, journals), web sites, online databases, films, television and radio broadcasts, compact discs, audiocassettes, record albums, dance performances, operas and other long musical compositions (except those identified simply by form, number, and key), works of visual art, ships, aircraft, and spacecraft.

1.5 Headings

- Numbered:
    - MLA recommends that when writing an essay into sections you number those sections with an Arabic number and a period followed by a space and the section name.
    - Example:

1. Soil Conservation
1.1 Erosion
1.2 Terracing
2. Water Conservation
3. Energy Conservation

- Unnumbered:
  - There are 5 unnumbered heading levels which are formatted as follows.
  - Example:

Level 1 Heading: bold, flush left

Level 2 Heading: italics, flush left

Level 3 Heading: centered, bold

Level 4 Heading: centered, italics

<u>Level 5 Heading: underlined, flush left</u>

	TABLE: MLA Headings
Level	Format
1	**Flush Left, Bold, Uppercase**
2	*Flush Left, Italics, Uppercase*
3	**Centered, Bold, Uppercase**
4	*Centered, Italics, Uppercase*
5	<u>Underlined, Flush Left, Regular, Uppercase</u>

1.6 Notes Page Layout

- Center the title "Notes," using 12-point Times New Roman font.
- Endnotes begin on a new page after the paper but before the Works Cited.
- Intend each entry 0.5 inch from the margin.

1.7 Works Cited Page Layout

- Works Cited starts on new page with heading.
- Center the title, Works Cited, an inch from the top of the page.
- 1" margins, double-spaced, 12-pt. font.
- Double-space between the title and the first entry.
- Hanging indent. Second and subsequent lines of citations indent 1.5" from margin.
- Each entry presents information in a specific order: the author's name, the title, the publication information.
- All citations are alphabetized by author's name.
- If two or more entries citing coauthors begin with the same name, alphabetize by the last names of the second authors listed.
- If the author's name is unknown, alphabetize by the title, ignoring any initial A, An, or The or the equivalent in another language.

2. Stylistic Technicalities

2.1 Abbreviations

2.1.1 Uppercase Letter Abbreviations

- Do not use periods or spaces in abbreviations composed solely of capital letters, except in the case of proper names:

US
MA
CD
HTML

2.1.2 Lowercase Letter Abbreviations

- Use a period if the abbreviation ends in a lowercase letter:

assn.
conf.
Eng.
esp.

- Referring to an Internet suffix, where the period should come before the abbreviation:

.com
.edu
.gov

- Degree names are a notable exception to the lowercase abbreviation rule:

  PhD
  EdD
  PsyD

- Use periods between letters without spacing if each letter represents a word in common lowercase abbreviations:

  a.m.
  e.g.
  i.e.

- Other notable exceptions:

  mph
  rpm
  ns
  lb

- Month names longer than four letters used in journal and magazine citations should be abbreviated:

  Jan.
  Feb.
  Mar.
  Apr.
  Aug.
  Sept.
  Oct.
  Nov.
  Dec.

- Abbreviate country, province, and state names:

Logan, UT
Manchester, Eng.
Sherbrooke, QC

- The list of common scholarly abbreviations:

anon. for anonymous
c. or ca. for circa
ch. for chapter
dept. for department
e.g. for example
ed. for edition
et al. for multiple names (translates to "and others")
fwd. for foreword
i.e. for that is
jour. for journal
lib. for library
no. for number
P for Press (used for academic presses)
p. for page, pp. for pages
par. for paragraph when page numbers are unavailable
qtd. in for quoted in
rev. for revised
sec. or sect. for section
ser. for series
trans. for translation
U for University (for example, Purdue U)
UP for University Press (for example, Yale UP or U of
California P)
var. for variant
vol. for volume

2.1.3 Exceptions:

- Omit articles and business abbreviations (like Corp., Inc., Co., and Ltd.).

- Use the acronym of the publisher if the company is commonly known by that abbreviation (e.g. MLA, ERIC, GPO).
- For publishers who are not known by an abbreviation, write the entire name.
- Use only U and P when referring to university presses (e.g. Cambridge UP or U of Arkansas P).

2.2 Footnotes and Endnotes

2.2.1 General

- Footnotes and endnotes for bibliographic notes refer to other publications readers may consult.
- Examples:

1. See Blackmur, especially chapters 3 and 4, for an insightful analysis of this trend.

2. On the problems related to repressed memory recovery, see Wollens 120-35; for a contrasting view, see Pyle 43; Johnson, Hull, Snyder 21-35; Krieg 78-91.

3. Several other studies point to this same conclusion. See Johnson and Hull 45-79, Kather 23-31, Krieg 50-57.

- Footnotes/content notes refer to brief additional information that might be too digressive for the main text.
- Example:

4. In a 1998 interview, she reiterated this point even more strongly: "I am an artist, not a politician!" (Weller 124).

2.2.2 Numbering Footnotes and Endnotes in Text

- Indicated in text by superscript Arabic numbers after the punctuation of the phrase to which the note refers.
- Examples:

Some have argued that such an investigation would be fruitless.[6]

Scholars have argued for years that this claim has no basis,[7] so we would do well to ignore it.

2.2.3 Footnotes

- Below the text body.
- MLA Handbook does not specify how to format footnotes.

2.2.4 Endnotes Page

- If you have any endnotes, include them on a separate page before your Works Cited page.
- Entitle the section Note(s):
  - o Centered
  - o Unformatted
- The first line of each endnote is indented five spaces, and subsequent lines are flush with the left margin.
- Place a period and a space after each endnote number, and then provide the appropriate note after the space.

2.3 Quotations

2.3.1 Short quotations

- Short quotations are four typed lines or fewer of prose or three lines of verse.
- Enclose the quotation within double quotation marks.
- Provide the author and specific page number (in the case of verse, provide line numbers) in the in-text citation.
- Include a complete reference on the Works Cited page.
- Punctuation marks such as periods, commas, and semicolons should appear after the parenthetical citation.
- Example:

According to some, dreams express "profound aspects of personality" (Foulkes 184), though others disagree.

According to Foulkes's study, dreams may express "profound aspects of personality" (184).

Is it possible that dreams may express "profound aspects of personality" (Foulkes 184)?

- When using short (fewer than three lines of verse) quotations from poetry, mark breaks in verse with a slash, (/), at the end of each line of verse.
- Example:

Cullen concludes, "Of all the things that happened there / That's all I remember" (11-12).

2.3.2 Long quotations

- For quotations that are more than four lines of prose or three lines of verse, place quotations in a free-standing block of text and omit quotation marks.
- Start the quotation on a new line, with the entire quote indented 1.5 inch from the left margin.
- Example:

Nelly Dean treats Heathcliff poorly and dehumanizes him throughout her narration:
They entirely refused to have it in bed with them, or even in their room, and I had no more sense, so, I put it on the landing of the stairs, hoping it would be gone on the morrow. By chance, or else attracted by hearing his voice, it crept to Mr. Earnshaw's door, and there he found it on quitting his chamber. Inquiries were made as to how it got there; I was obliged to confess, and in recompense for my cowardice and inhumanity was sent out of the house. (Bronte 78)

- When citing long sections of poetry (four lines of verse or more), keep formatting as close to the original as possible.
- Example:

In his poem "My Papa's Waltz," Theodore Roethke explores his childhood with his father:

The whiskey on your breath
Could make a small boy dizzy;
But I hung on like death:
Such waltzing was not easy.
We Romped until the pans
Slid from the kitchen shelf;
My mother's countenance
Could not unfrown itself. (qtd. in Shrodes, Finestone, Shugrue 202)

- When citing two or more paragraphs, use block quotation format.
- The first line of the second paragraph should be indented an extra 0.25 inch to denote a new paragraph:

2.3.2 Adding or Omitting Words in Quotations

- Put brackets around the words to indicate that they are not part of the original text.
- Example:

Jan Harold Brunvand, in an essay on urban legends, states, "some individuals [who retell urban legends] make a point of learning every rumor or tale" (78).

- If you omit word(s) from a quotation, you should indicate the deleted word or words by using (. . .)
- Example:

In an essay on urban legends, Jan Harold Brunvand notes that "some individuals make a point of learning every recent rumor or tale . . . and in a short time a lively exchange of details occurs" (78).

- When omitting one or more full lines of poetry, space several periods to about the length of a complete line in the poem.
- Example:

These beauteous forms,
Through a long absence, have not been to me
As is a landscape to a blind man's eye:
. . . .
Felt in the blood, and felt along the heart;
And passing even into my purer mind,
With tranquil restoration . . . (22-24, 28-30)

3. Citing Sources

3.1 In-Text Citations

3.1.1 General

- Provide relevant source information in parentheses whenever a sentence uses a quotation or paraphrase.
- Any source information that you provide in-text must correspond to the source information on the Works Cited page:
    - Whatever signal word or phrase you provide to your readers in the text must be the first thing that appears on the left-hand margin of the corresponding entry on the Works Cited page.
- Put the author's name and the page number in parentheses.
- If there is no author or the author is an organization, use an abbreviated version of the title instead.
- If there is no page number, you can usually just list the author.
- If you are citing the work as a whole, rather than a quote or fact from a specific page, you do not need to include a page number.
- Another option is to mention the author's name in a signal phrase in your text, in which case you can just put the page number, if there is one, at the end of the sentence.

3.1.2 Authors

- In most cases, the Parenthetical References include the author's last name and the specific page number for the information cited.
- Author's name in text.
  - When you use the author's name in your text in citing a reference, give only the page number.
  - Example:

Magny develops this argument (67-69).

- Author's name in parenthetical reference.
  - When the author's name is not in your text, add the author's last name in parentheses.
  - Example:

This argument has been developed (Magny 67-69).

- No author's name.
  - If no author's name is given, abbreviate the title and add the page number.
  - Example:

(Other Pole 33).

- Two or more authors.
  - If the source has two or three authors, include all last names.
  - Example:

(Gibson and Stabler 727).
(Sumner, Reichl, and Waugh 23).

- If the source has more than three authors, include the first author, followed by et al.
  - Example:

(Leikin et al. 67).

- Corporate author.
  - Use the same format, but include the corporate body.
  - Example:

(Modern Language Association 77).

- More than one work by the same author.
  - Abbreviate the title. For example, if you use two sources by Shakespeare, Comedy of Errors and Ages of Man, then you will include the following.
  - Example:

(Shakespeare, Comedy 54).
(Shakespeare, Ages 25).

  - If you state the author's name in the text, give only the title and page number in parentheses.
  - Example:

(Comedy 54).

- Multivolume works.
  - When citing a volume number and a page reference, separate the two by a colon and a space.
  - Omit the words volume and page or their abbreviations.
  - Example:

(Henderson 3: 52).
(Wellek 2: 1-10).

  - When referring to an entire volume, use only volume number. Place a comma after the

author's name and include the abbreviation "vol.".
- o Example:

(Henderson, vol. 3).

- o In text reference to an entire volume.
- o Example:

In volume 3, Henderson suggests …

- More than one work in parenthetical reference.
  - o Cite each work as you would in a reference and use semicolons to separate the citations.
  - o Example:

This controversy has been addressed more than once (Dabundo 27; Magny 69).

- Electronic and online sources.
  - o Cite them just like print sources.
  - o If an online source lacks numbering, omit numbers.
  - o If a source includes fixed page numbers or section numbering, such as numbering paragraphs (pars.), screens (screens) or chapters (ch.), cite the relevant numbers.
  - o Example:

The semiconductor workplace is highly toxic (Ross par. 35).

Beethoven has been called the "first politically motivated composer," for he was "caught
up in the whole ferment of ideas that came out of the French Revolution" (Gardiner screens 2-3).

"Once we start using a tool extensively, it also starts using us" (Rawlins ch. 1, sec. 1).

3.1.3 Specific Sources

- Citing the Bible
  - In your first parenthetical citation, you want to make clear which Bible you're using (underline or italicize the title), as each version varies in its translation, followed by book (do not italicize or underline), chapter, and verse.
  - Example:

Ezekiel saw "what seemed to be four living creatures," each with faces of a man, a lion, an ox, and an eagle (*New Jerusalem Bible*, Ezek. 1.5-10).

  - If future references employ the same edition of the Bible you're using, list only the book, chapter, and verse in the parenthetical citation.
  - Example:

John of Patmos echoes this passage when describing his vision (Rev. 4.6-8).

3.1.4 Examples

Source	In-Text	Woks Cited
Source with one author	Mushanga believes that all crimes fall into one of three categories (13). Based on the three categories of crime (Mushanga 13)...	Mushanga, Tibamanya Mwene. "Political Crimes." *Crime and Deviance: An Introduction to Criminology*, Law Africa, 2011, pp.27-35. *Ebrary*.
Source with	Dubner and Levitt reject that assertion	Dubner, Stephen J., and Steven Levitt.

two authors	(229), and suggest instead… That assertion has been rejected (Dubner and Levitt 229), replaced with the notion that…	*Freakonomics: A Rogue Economist Explores the Hidden Side of Everything.* Turtleback Books, 2009.
Source with more than two authors	Emergency departments around the country faced significant increases in intakes in the year 2014 (Gonzalez Morganti, et al.). According to Gonzalez Morganti, et al., the results were unequivocal.	Gonzalez Morganti, Kristy, et al. "The Evolving Role of Emergency Departments in the United States." *Journal of Emergency Care*, vol. 45, no.2, Aug. 2015. *Academic Search Complete.*
Source with no author	The book even made it to the top of many publishers' favorites list in 2013 ("Staff Picks").	"Staff Picks 2013." *Publisher's Weekly*, 6 May 2013, vol.260, no. 18, pp.26-28. *Literature Resource Center.*
Source with no page numbers	Some officials even plan on using shaming as a tactic to get mortgage lenders to respond (Powell). According to Powell, some officials even plan on using shaming as a tactic to get mortgage lenders to respond.	Powell, Michael. "Billions to Fight Foreclosure, but Few New Loans." *The New York Times*, 29 Dec. 2009, www.nytimes.com/2009/12/30/nyregion/30foreclose.html.

Source with no author and no page numbers	Medical professionals around the country have described childhood obesity is described as a "serious medical condition" ("Childhood Obesity").	"Childhood Obesity: Definition." *Mayo Clinic*, 3 Nc 2015, www.mayoclinic.org/disease: conditions/childhood-obesity/basics/definition/con- 20027428.

3.2 Works Cited

3.2.1 General

- Works Cited starts on new page with heading.
- Center the title, Works Cited, an inch from the top of the page.
- 1" margins, double-spaced, 12-pt. font.
- Double-space between the title and the first entry.
- Hanging indent. Second and subsequent lines of citations indent 1.5" from margin.
- Each entry presents information in a specific order: the author's name, the title, the publication information.
- All citations are alphabetized by author's name.
- If only one page of a print source is used, mark it with the abbreviation "p." before the page number (e.g., p.157).
- If a span of pages is used, mark it with the abbreviation "pp." before the page number (e.g., pp.157-168).
- Capitalize each word in the titles of articles, books, etc, but do not capitalize articles (the, an), prepositions, or conjunctions unless one is the first word of the title or

subtitle: Gone with the Wind, The Art of War, There Is Nothing Left to Lose.
- Use italics (instead of underlining) for titles of larger works (books, magazines) and quotation marks for titles of shorter works (poems, articles).
- For online sources:
  - Omit "http://" from the address.
  - The date of access is optional.
- All works cited entries end with a period.

3.2.2 Authors

- If two or more entries citing coauthors begin with the same name, alphabetize by the last names of the second authors listed.
- To cite two or more works by the same author, give the name in the first entry only. In all following entries, place three hyphens in place of the name.
  - Example:

Meyer, Stephanie. *Eclipse.* 1st ed., Little, Brown, 2007.
- - - . *Breaking Dawn.* 1st ed., Little, Brown, 2008.

- When an author or collection editor appears both as the sole author of a text and as the first author of a group, list solo-author entries first.
  - Example:

Heller, Steven, ed. *The Education of an E-Designer.*
Heller, Steven, and Karen Pomeroy. *Design Literacy: Understanding Graphic Design.*

- If the author's name is unknown, alphabetize by the title, ignoring any initial A, An, or The or the equivalent in another language.

3.2.3 Specific Sources

- The Bible.
  - Italicize "The Bible" and follow it with the version you are using.
- Example:

The Bible. Authorized King James Version, Oxford UP, 1998.

The Bible. The New Oxford Annotated Version, 3rd ed., Oxford UP, 2001.

The New Jerusalem Bible. Edited by Susan Jones, Doubleday, 1985.

3.2.4 General Template

Source	Works Cited Template
Entire Book	Author last name, first name. *Book Title: With Subtitle if Present.* Publisher Name, Year.
Book Chapter	Last name, first name. "Chapter Title." *Book Title: With Subtitle if Present,* Publisher Name, Year, pp.#-#.
Edited Book	Editor last name, first name, editor. *Book Title: With Subtitle if Present.* Publisher Name, Year.
Printed article (not available online or in a database)	Last name, First name. "Article Title." *Publication Title,* vol.#, no.#, Day Mon. Year, pp.#- #.

Magazine, Newspaper or Journal Article from a SCC library database	Last name, First name. "Article Title." *Publication Title,* vol.#, no.#, Day Mon. Year, pp.#- #. Database Name.
Magazine, Newspaper, or Journal Article from the Internet	Last name, First name. "Article Title." *Publication Title,* vol.#, no.#, Day Mon. Year, www.resourceURL.com OR doi:#.
Electronic Book from the Internet	Author last name, first name. *Book Title: With Subtitle if Present.* Publisher Name, Year, *Name of Organization Providing Book,* www.resourceURL.com.
Webpage	Last name, first name (if present). "Webpage Title." *Website Name,* Publisher Name (omit if same as website name), Day Mon. Year published (if present), www.resourceURL.com.
Online video from YouTube or other video hosting site	Creator name. "Video Title." *Website Name,* Publisher Name (omit if same as website name), Day Mon. Year published (if present), www.resourceURL.com.

3.2.5 Other Sources Examples

Source	Works Cited Example
Article from the web‡	Manne, Kate. "Why I Use Trigger Warnings." *The New York Times*, 19 Sept. 2015, www.nytimes.com/2015/09/20/opinion/sund ay/why-i-use-trigger-warnings.html.

Book	Moore, Jamillah. *Race and College Admissions: A Case for Affirmative Action.* McFarland, 2005.
Custom course text or other anthology	Rousseau, Jean-Jacques. Excerpt from *The Social Contract.* Translated by Maurice Cranston, 1968. *Western Tradition II,* Saint Mary's College of California, 2014, pp. 130-44.
Document from the web	United States, National Institutes of Health. *Cancer and the Environment: What You Need to Know, What You Can Do. National Institute of Environmental Health Sciences,* 2003, www.niehs.nih.gov/health/materials/cancer _and_the_environment_508.pdf.
E-book (3+ authors) from a database	Safir, Marilyn P., et al., editors. *Future Directions in Post-Traumatic Stress Disorder: Prevention, Diagnosis, and Treatment.* 3rd ed., Springer, 2015. *SpringerLink,* link.springer.com/book/10.1007%2F978-1-4899-7522-5.
Encyclopedi a article from a database	Debinski, Diane M., and Molly S. Cross. "Conservation and Global Climate Change." *The Princeton Guide to Ecology,* edited by Simon A. Levin et al., 3rd ed., Princeton UP, 2012. *Credo Reference,* stmarys-ca.idm.oclc.org/login?url=http://literati.credo reference.com/content/entry/prge/conservat ion_and_global_climate_change/0.
Journal article from a database*	Pope, H. Lavar. "Hyphy Rap Music, Cooptation, and Black Fanatics in Oakland, CA." *Souls,* vol. 16, no. 3-4, 2014, pp. 242-268. *Taylor & Francis Online,* doi: 10.1080/10999949.2014.970471.
Webpage or	Hollmichel, Stefanie. "The Reading Brain:

blog	Differences between Digital and Print." *So Many Books*, 25 Apr. 2013, somanybooksblog.com/2013/04/25/the-reading-brain-differences-between-digital-and-print.
YouTube (or other online) video	"Rudy Giuliani Doubles Down on Clinton Health Conspiracy." *Fox News Sunday*, 21 Aug. 2016. *YouTube*, uploaded by TP Clips, 21 Aug. 2016, www.youtube.com/watch?v=u3pKTn_rNBI.
Tweet	@persiankiwi. "We have report of large street battles in east & west of Tehran now - #Iranelection." *Twitter*, 23 June 2009, 11:15 a.m., twitter.com/persiankiwi/status/2298106072.

3.3 In-Text and Woks Cited Examples

Source	Works Cited	In-Text
Book, One Author	Alexis, Andre. *Fifteen Dogs: An Apologue*. Coach House Books, 2015.	(Alexis 58)
Book, Two Authors	Lutgens, Frederick K., and Edward J. Tarbuck. *The Atmosphere: An Introduction to Meteorology*. 13th ed., Pearson, 2016.	(Lutgens and Tarbuck 219)
Book, Edited	Bartol, Curt R., and Anne M. Bartol, editors. *Current Perspectives in Forensic Psychology and Criminal Behavior*. 4th ed., Sage, 2016.	(Bartol and Bartol 78)

Book, Corporate Author	Canadian Health Information Management Association. *Fundamentals of Health Information Management.* Canadian Healthcare Association, 2013	(Canadian Health Information Management Association 87)
Book, No Author	*American Heritage Dictionary for Learners of English.* Houghton, 2002.	(American Heritage 49)
Book, Three or More Authors	Guttman, B., et al. *Genetics: A Beginner's Guide.* Oneworld, 2002.	(Guttman et al. 77)
Book, Online	Shaw, Bernard. *Pygmalion.* Brentano, 1916. *Bartleby.com,* http://www.bartleby.com/138/. Accessed 14 Jan. 2018.	(Shaw)
Library eBook	Fraihat, I. *Unfinished revolutions: Yemen, Libya, and Tunisia after the Arab Spring.* Yale UP, 2016. *ebrary,* orca.douglascollege.ca/record= b1940699~S9. Accessed 14 Nov. 2016.	(Fraihat 76)
Encyclopedia or Dictionary Entry, (Online) with an Author	Friesen, Gerald. "Assiniboia." *The Canadian Encyclopedia,* 3 Apr. 2015, *Historica Canada.* www.thecanadianencyclopedia .com/en/article/assiniboia/. Accessed 29 July 2016.	(Friesen)
Encyclopedia or	"Maelstrom." Merriam-Webster Dictionary, 2017, *Merriam-*	("Maelstrom")

Dictionary Entry, (Online) without an Author	*Webster*. www.merriam-webster.com/dictionary/maelstrom. Accessed 19 Oct. 2016.	
Encyclopedia or Dictionary Entry, (Print) with an Author	Lewisohn, Leonard. "Sufism." *Encyclopedia of Philosophy*, edited by Donald Borchert, 2nd ed., vol. 9, Thomson Gale, 2006, pp. 300-314.	(Lewisohn, 307)
Encyclopedia or Dictionary Entry, (Print) without an Author	"Mystic." *Oxford Concise Dictionary of Phrase and Fable*, edited by Elizabeth Knowles, Oxford UP, 2003, p. 349.	("Mystic" 349)
Journal, Article (print)	Conatser, Phillip, and Martin Block. "Aquatic Instructors' Beliefs Toward Inclusion." *Therapeutic Recreation Journal*, vol. 35, no. 2, 2001, pp. 170-184.	(Conatser and Block 177)
Journal, Article from a Library Database without a DOI	Williams, George R. "What Can Consciousness Anomalies Tell Us about Quantum Mechanics?" *Journal of Scientific Exploration*, vol.30, no. 3, 2015, pp. 326-354. *Academic Search Complete*, 0-search. ebscohost.com.orca.douglasco	(Williams 344)

	llege.ca/login.aspx?direct=true &db =a9h&AN=118525144&site=eh ost-live&scope=site. Accessed 6 Nov. 2016.	
Journal, Article from a Library Database with a DOI (Multiple Authors)	Rabb, Nathaniel, et al. "Truths About Beauty and Goodness: Disgust Affects Moral but not Aesthetic Judgments." *Psychology of Aesthetics, Creativity and the Arts*, vol. 10, no. 4, 2016, pp. 492-500. *PsycINFO*, doi:10.1037/aca0000051. Accessed 12 Nov. 2016.	(Rabb et al. 494)
Journal, Article from the Internet	Cianciolo, Patricia K. "Compensating Nuclear Weapons Workers and Their Survivors: The Case of Fernald." Michigan Family Review, vol. 19, no. 1, 2015, pp. 51-72, quod.lib.umich.edu/m/mfr/4919 087.0019.103?rgn=main;view= fulltext. Accessed 21 Sept. 2016.	(Cianciolo 61)
Website	Galewitz, Phil. "In Depressed Rural Kentucky, Worries Mount Over Medicaid Cutbacks." *NPR*, 19 Nov. 2016, www.npr.org/sections/health-shots/2016/11/19/502580120/i n-depressed-rural-kentucky-worries-mount-over-medicaid-cutbacks. Accessed 21 Nov.	(Galewitz)

	2016.	
Wikipedia , Articles	"Hypnosis." *Wikipedia*, 26 Nov. 2016, en.wikipedia.org/wiki/Hypnosis. Accessed 26 Nov. 2016.	("Hypnosis")
Blog Post	Minchilli, Elizabeth. "Eating Outside in Rome." *Elizabeth Minchilli in Rome*, 13 April 2016, www.elizabethminchilliinrome.com/2016/04/eating-outside-rome/. Accessed 18 July 2016.	(Minchilli)
Governm ent Documen t Where the Author is also the Publisher	*Canada's Greenhouse Gas Emissions: Understanding the Trends, 1990-2006.* Environment Canada, 2008, publications.gc.ca/collections/collection_2009/ec/En81-4-2006-2E.pdf. Accessed 19 Jan. 2017.	(Canada's Greenhouse 17)
Governm ent Documen t - Print	*Information Use by the Ministry of Health in Resource Allocation Decisions for the Regional Health Care System.* Office of the Auditor General of British Columbia, 2002.	(Information Use 22)
Film	*The Grand Budapest Hotel.* Directed by Wes Anderson. Performance by Ralph Fiennes, Twentieth Century Fox Home Entertainment, 2014.	(*Grand Budapest* 01:18:29-49)

Streaming Video from a Website, YouTube etc.	Griggs, Ben. "A Day in the Life of a Librarian." *YouTube*, 1 Oct. 2013, www.youtube.com/watch?v=Mcn-B7X7HwQ. Accessed 9 Oct. 2017.	(Griggs 00:02:26-27)
CD	Tragically Hip. *Road Apples.* MCA Records, 19	(Tragically Hip)
Song on a CD	Cohen, Leonard. "Jazz Police." *I'm Your Man.* Columbia, 1988.	(Cohen)
Photograph (Web)	Dobbs, Charles. "Zabriskie Point Sunset." *FineArtAmerica*, 7 Apr. 2016, fineartamerica.com/featured/zabriskie-point-sunset-charles-dobbs.html. Accessed 16 Dec. 2016.	(Dobbs)
Podcast Reference Kennedy	Kennedy, Paul. "Hope Within Horror: Marina Nemat." *Ideas*, CBC/Radio-Canada, 6 Dec. 2016, www.cbc.ca/radio/ideas/hope-within-horror-marina-nemat-1.3470823. Accessed 12 Dec. 2016.	(Kennedy 00:14:11-47)
Lectures, Speeches or Readings	Cannon, Dolores. "Psychology 406: Accessing Theta." 28 Oct. 2016, Douglas College, New Westminster. Class lecture.	(Cannon)

Interviews Conducted by Yourself	Rewniak, Christopher. Personal Interview. 4 June 2017.	(Rewniak)
Brochures/Pamphlets	*Not Everyone Has a Home.* National Coalition for the Homeless. Pamphlet.	(Not Everyone)
Email	Selig, Pauline. "Re: Knowledge topics." Received by Russell Moore, 22 July 2016.	(Selig)
Tweet	@persiankiwi. "We have report of large street battles in east & west of Tehran now - #Iranelection." *Twitter*, 23 June 2009, 11:15 a.m., twitter.com/persiankiwi/status/2298106072.	(@persiankiwi)

4. Tables, Figures, and Examples

4.1 General

- There three types of visuals/illustrations: tables, figures, examples.
- The illustration label and number should always appear in two places:
  - the document main text (see fig. 1),
  - near the illustration itself (Fig. 1.).
- Captions provide titles.
- Example:

Fig. 1. Van Gogh's The Starry Night

4.2 Tables

- Refer to the table and its corresponding numeral in-text:
  - Do not capitalize the word table (e.g. "(see table 2)").
- Align the table flush-left to the margin.
- Label the table 'Table' and provide its corresponding Arabic numeral. No punctuation is necessary after the label and number.
- On the next line, provide a caption for the table:
  - Use title case.
- Place the table below the caption, flush-left.
- Below the title, signal the source information with the descriptor "Source"

- o If you provide source information with your illustrations, you do not need to provide this information on the Works Cited page.

- In-test example:

In 1985, women aged 65 and older were 59% more likely than men of the same age to reside in a nursing home, and though 11,700 less women of that age group were enrolled in 1999, men over the same time period ranged from 30,000 to 39,000 persons while women accounted for 49,000 to 61,500 (see table 1).

- Caption Example:

Table 1
Rate of Nursing Home Residence among People Age 65 or Older, by Sex and Age Group, 1985, 1995, 1997, 1999.

Example Table

Source: Federal Interagency Forum on Aging-Related Statistics, *Older Americans 2008: Key Indicators of Well-Being,* Federal Interagency Forum on Aging-Related Statistics, Mar. 2008, table 35A.

4.3 Figures

- All visuals/illustrations that are not tables are labeled Figure or Fig.

- Refer to the figure in-text and provide an Arabic numeral that corresponds to the figure:
  - Do not capitalize figure or fig.
- Below the figure, provide a label name and its corresponding arabic numeral (e.g. Fig. 1.).
- Beginning with the same line as the label and number, provide a title and/or caption as well as relevant source information in note form.
  - If you provide source information with your illustrations, you do not need to provide this information on the Works Cited page.

- In-text example:

Some readers found Harry's final battle with Voldemort a disappointment, and recently, the podcast, MuggleCast debated the subject (see fig. 2).

- Caption Example:

Fig. 2. Harry Potter and Voldemort final battle debate from Andrew Sims et al.; "Show 166"; MuggleCast; MuggleNet.com, 19 Dec. 2008, www.mugglenet.com/2015/11/the-snape-debate-rowling-speaks-out.

4.4 Examples

- The descriptor "Example" refers to musical illustrations (e.g. portions of a musical score). It is often abbreviated "ex."
- Refer to the example in-text and provide an Arabic numeral.
    - Do not capitalize "example" or "ex" in the text.
- Below the example, provide the label (capitalizing Example or Ex.), number, and a caption or title.
    - If you provide source information with your illustrations, you do not need to provide this information on the Works Cited page.

- In-text example:

In Ambroise Thomas's opera *Hamlet,* the title character's iconic theme first appears in Act 1. As Hamlet enters the castle's vacant grand hall following his mother's coronation, the low strings begin playing the theme (ex 1).

- Caption Example:

Ex. 1: Hamlet's Theme

Source: Thomas, Ambroise. *Hamlet*. 1868.

5. Paper Layout Example

Student's Name Surname

Professor's Name Surname

Course

Day Month Year

The Title of Paper

First Level Heading

Lorem ipsum dolor sit amet, porro ullum ne sea, ad vis odio decore. Ne corrumpit gubergren referrentur nec, sed cu quot causae sententiae. Quodsi eleifend pri ut. Ei lobortis iracundia pri. Euismod hendrerit repudiandae nec at.

Second Level Heading

Lorem ipsum dolor sit amet, porro ullum ne sea, ad vis odio decore. Ne corrumpit gubergren referrentur nec, sed cu quot causae sententiae. Quodsi eleifend pri ut. Ei lobortis iracundia pri. Euismod hendrerit repudiandae nec at.

Third Level Heading

Lorem ipsum dolor sit amet, porro ullum ne sea, ad vis odio decore. Ne corrumpit gubergren referrentur nec, sed cu quot causae sententiae. Quodsi eleifend pri ut. Ei lobortis iracundia pri. Euismod hendrerit repudiandae nec at.

Fourth Level Heading

Lorem ipsum dolor sit amet, porro ullum ne sea, ad vis odio decore. Ne lobortis iracundia pri. Euismod hendrerit repudiandae nec at.

Fifth Level Heading

Lorem ipsum dolor sit amet, porro ullum ne sea, ad vis odio decore. Ne lobortis iracundia pri. Euismod hendrerit repudiandae nec at.

---- (new page) ---

Notes

1. Danhof includes "Delaware, Maryland, all states north of the Potomac and Ohio rivers, Missouri, and states to its north" when referring to the northern states (11).

2. For the purposes of this paper, "science" is defined as it was in nineteenth century agriculture: conducting experiments and engaging in research.

3. Please note that any direct quotes from the nineteenth century texts are written in their original form, which may contain grammar mistakes according to twenty-first century grammar rules.

Works Cited

"Childhood Obesity: Definition." *Mayo Clinic*, 3 Nov. 2015,

www.mayoclinic.org/diseases-

conditions/childhood-obesity/basics/definition/con-20027428.

Dubner, Stephen J., and Steven Levitt. *Freakonomics: A

Rogue Economist Explores the Hidden Side of

Everything.* Turtleback Books, 2009.

Gonzalez Morganti, Kristy, et al. "The Evolving Role of

Emergency Departments in the United States." *Journal

of Emergency Care*, vol. 45, no.2, Aug. 2015.

Academic Search Complete.

Mushanga, Tibamanya Mwene. "Political Crimes." *Crime and

Deviance: An Introduction to Criminology*, Law Africa,

2011, pp.27-35. *Ebrary*.

Powell, Michael. "Billions to Fight Foreclosure, but Few New

Loans." *The New York Times*, 29 Dec. 2009,

www.nytimes.com/2009/12/30/nyregion/30foreclose.ht
ml.

"Staff Picks 2013." *Publisher's Weekly*, 6 May 2013, vol.260,
no. 18, pp.26-28. *Literature Resource Center.*

Sources

1. MLA Handbook, 8th ed. PN 147 G525 2016

2. MLA Style Manual and Guide to Scholarly Publishing. 3rd ed. PN 147 M527 2008

CPSIA information can be obtained
at www.ICGtesting.com
Printed in the USA
BVHW042137050220
571605BV00012B/114